The Little Book of
DRINKING

D1459211

The Little Book of
DRINKING

Probably the Best Book
in the World

DR MARC BLAKE

BOXTREE

First published 2002 by Boxtree
an imprint of Pan Macmillan Ltd
Pan Macmillan, 20 New Wharf Road, London N1 9RR
Basingstoke and Oxford
Associated companies throughout the world
www.panmacmillan.com

ISBN 0 7522 1503 5

9 8 7 6 5 4 3 2 1

A CIP catalogue record for this book is available from
the British Library.

Design by seagulls
Printed and bound in Great Britain by Cox and Wyman Ltd,
Reading, Berkshire

INTRODUCTION

The Little book of Drinking is packed full of interesting stuff that you can go on and on about in some dingy pub until even your best mates (who hate you anyway) pour their pints over your head.

Learn about

- Drinker's roulette (spin the room not the bottle).

- Drunk etiquette (should I vomit on my partner or try for the toilet?).

- Poor man's cocktails (anything found in the slops bucket).

- How to break the ice at parties (start a fight in the coatroom).

It's all a bit of fun. Go on – 'ave a larfff. Y'bastarrrrddd. G'wannnn. Arrghhh . . .

So –
if you're able to read this, and you can remember what the hell you're doing in a book or record shop anyway – then ish for you.

And remember: there are happy drunks, maudlin drunks and there is you, you sad, sick perverted son of a bitch. Fancy a pint?

DRINK SLANG

Hammered/lashed/slaughtered/
caned/on the piss/mullered/pie-
eyed/on a session/off for a quick
one/a swift half/a snifter/three
sheets to the wind/a small
libation/one for the road/a wee
dram/wetting my whistle/a
bijou drinkette/see a man about
a dog/piss-up/night out/painting
the town red/wetting the baby's
head/knocking one back/getting
one in/quenching a thirst/
having a serious drink . . .
– all these are likely to get you
stopped on the way home by a
man in a nice big blue helmet.

PUBS TO AVOID – AND THEIR INHABITANTS

Pubs that won't serve you in jeans

Sure sign that they are trying to appeal to women who you don't have a chance of sleeping with. That or it wants to be a wine bar.

Gastro-Pubs

Offer a selection of Frenchie foods and have poncy menus on the tables. This is all getting in the way of the DRINKING!

Pubs with big hungry dogs

Just don't – all right?

Pubs with 'comedy' names

The Geese and Chiropractor,
the Drink Inn, the Wet Whistle.
These are run by landlords
with failed marriages and
moustaches and appeal only to
middle-aged couples with a
sense of humour failure.

Pubs with Olde Worlde Graphics

This sign wasn't really written by a medieval peasant, was it? No – it was some brewery marketing department twat – that or the landlord's dimwit son who thinks he's going to get a grant to go to art school.

Pubs that do coffee

No. No. No no no no no no no.
We do not want the poison and
the cure next to each other,
thank you. It's like a beautiful
woman – with scabs.

Pubs with these names

The Brokers' Rest.
The Glass-in-Face.
The Screaming Liver.
The Fox and Stomach-pump.

OTHER PUBS YOU SHOULD AVOID – AND WHAT TO SPOT IN THEM
(5 points each)

STUDENT PUB

Students . . . Bloody students.

No traffic cones in a mile radius.

MTV on loud enough to drown out Concorde.

Plastic pint glasses that split when carried from the bar.

Barmaids with coloured fingernails (which will end up in your drink).

Graffiti about bands you have never heard of and never will again.

Small 'wraps' and pieces of silver paper abandoned when anyone over twenty-five comes in.

Cheap nasty lager.

Rizla packets with bits torn off.

OLD MAN PUB

Phlegm.

Copy of *Racing Post* and/or *Express* abandoned on bar (with the crossword filled in).

Halves of mild.

Smoke.

Bit quiet in here, innit?

IRISH THEME PUB

Instruments tacked to the
walls with names you cannot
pronounce and that no one
has played since the
Troubles began.

No one Irish.

19

And we're not in
Ireland, are we?

Charity collections
for 'the Cause'.

Black drinks that take four
days to pour and turn
your stools black.

Aussie barmaids.

AUSSIE PUB

Vomit on floor.

No apparent hygiene.

More bloody Aussie – and
Kiwi – barmaids. Christ!

Rugby players.

Sticky. Everywhere.

Ocker music on the jukebox.
AC/DC. Crowded House.
Ryan Adams.

COUNTRY PUB

Old toff still expecting drinks on the slate.

Snacks that are suspiciously 'natural'.

Dogs that may actually be werewolves.

Horse brasses and Olde Worlde maps of when this was all fields.

Old Bint who is 'quite a character', and who regularly pisses herself.

Lary young farmers tanked on cider and up for a fight.

SEASIDE PUB

Skol. Harp. Watneys Red
Barrel. Big D Peanuts circa 1976

Ruddy-cheeked yokels
(and they'll show you
them if you pay).

Fifteen-year-old girls trying
to get up the duff.

All-permeating stink of fish.

Bits of net and driftwood and
a ship's wheel nailed up.

A shit in a bottle.

A hidden sign that tells you
to 'mind your head' on the
way down to the stinking bogs.

HOW MUCH OF A DRINKER ARE YOU? IT'S TOO MUCH IF...

The council gives you
your own bottle bank.

You regularly hold onto
the floor to stop yourself
sliding off the Earth.

There are cleaning products
missing from your home.

Every photo of you has red-eye and there's nothing wrong with the camera.

You celebrate every day because – 'Hey, *someone's* got a birthday.'

Your most stable relationships are with kebabs, bollards and the local magistrate.

It's all gone. Wife, dog . . .
bowel control.

You know you've been sick
but you can't be arsed to
go and find it.

You're number 1 on the AA's
most wanted list.

You sing 'Danny Boy' and
you aren't even Irish.

You break up a children's game of spin-the bottle by screaming 'Sacrilege!'

You're asked to blow up the balloons for a party and you reach for a mint.

You know every pub in town – and have been thrown out of all of them.

Drinking myth no.1.

A barman will always listen to hard-luck stories. Barmen *are* hard-luck stories. Why else would they be working eighteen hours a day in a darkened room?

Drinking myth no.2.

Drink provokes the desire but takes away the performance. Who gives a shit about performance?

Drinking myth no.3.

You can drink yourself sober. It's *true*, Occifer. I heard it in the paaab.

The Legendary Drinker's Roll of Honour

In reverse order . . .

5. Herve Villechaize. A dwarf (who drank shorts, naturally) used to regularly drink his own weight in booze and go whoring around LA nightspots dressed as John Travolta. Threatened a 6 foot 3 inch bailiff who tried to serve him a court order – and then drank himself to death. Look, boss – pissed again.

4. Dylan Thomas. Welsh poet who avoided conscription by turning up so hammered that he was medically unfit to serve. Drank his way from Swansea to Soho. Pegged out at thirty-nine.

3. Vaclav Havel. President of Czechoslovakia – and you try saying that when you've had a couple. Skipped functions to get sloshed. Hired Frank Zappa as cultural attaché.

2. George Best. Legendarily pissed it up the wall. Debuted at Man United at the age of seventeen and squandered his talent in nightclubs before retiring at twenty-six. Served two months of a jail term for drink-driving and assaulting a copper. The most naturally gifted footballer of his generation, he's more remembered for appearing pissed on *Wogan*. Has now had his stomach stapled and can never drink again.
But he will.
Oh, he will.

1. Oliver Reed. A man who even now is challenging the devil to a yard-of-brimstone competition. Olly collapsed and died in a bar in Malta. He once drank 104 pints in an arm-wrestling competition in Guernsey. In his will he put £10,000 behind the bar of his local. But only for people who cried.

Also please make room at the bar for . . . Dean Martin, Errol Flynn. George Washington. Henry VIII, Maradona and Gazza. And your dad. Probably.

The Serious Drinker's Diary

7 a.m. Wake up. Are you kidding? The only way I'd be awake at 7 a.m. is if I was still on a bender or coming out of a coma in a casualty ward a hundred miles from home . . . wherever home is.

10 a.m. Still not paying attention, are you? I'm asleep in my vom-stained clothes and sheets or – if in park – am now being roused by foraging animals. One hour until opening time. First sign of life. My breath scares off the local dogs.

11.30 a.m. Kick-start the day with a pint to banish guilt and recriminations about choice of lifestyle and emptiness of human existence. Then – Breakfast of Champions. Packet of Hula-Hoops!

1.45pm. Ejected from hostelry for leering at PA girlies on their lunch break and whispering such endearments as 'You're all whoresons and bitches.' Decide on perambulation in the direction of the town centre.

2 p.m. Post off-licence visit,
I hook up with some gentlemen
friends on the bench outside
the library. A lively discussion
ensues as to relative merits of
Red Stripe and Special Brew,
ending up with a windmill fight
and a warning to move on.

5 p.m. Serious drinking begins. Despite all-day opening hours being commonplace I still find it necessary to follow some kind of schedule. Or pub-crawl. Choice of libation. Beer, with whisky chasers. Or whisky with beer chasers. Whogivesafuck?

7.30 p.m. UB cheque is at its lowest ebb and need to call in some favours. Ex-wife and children none too happy about my screaming obscenities outside their new home. Her bloke threatens the law. I counter with an offer to leave peaceably for a score. He offers a tenner and kick up the arse. Result!

9 p.m. Celebrate good fortune in a local tavern. I prefer pubs with sports on TV as communal atmosphere often means I can piggyback on rounds with my new-found beered-up best mates. Am as delighted as they are when Real Madrid scores. Or Chelsea. Or Tiger Woods. Or Batman.

11.30 p.m. My new best friends bid me a cheery farewell in the bins behind the chip shop. Time for a club or lock-in as am developing quite a thirst.

12.30 a.m. Effect entrance to cheapest nightspot on outskirts of town. Seems my trouserage is so begrimed the bouncer couldn't tell it was once denim. I meet a desirable woman. When I ask her if she's testing products for the cosmetic industry and it *doesn't* produce a slap – I know I'm on!

1 a.m. Brilliant. She drinks as much as me and my suggestion of vodka cocktails with rude names goes down a treat.
Life is a gift.

1.20 a.m. We're out of cash and the credit card she 'found' has been refused. Still. Nerys is still up for it. She's even offered to show me her op scars back at hers.

2 a.m. She attributes my
lack of response to the drink.
I attribute it to the fact that
she is really an ex-trucker from
Durham. I steal the contents
of her drinks cabinet on the
way out. After all, she's
been rifling through my
cabinet, so fair's fair.

48

2.15 a.m. The happiest vowels are A and E and here I am again. I fall into a grateful sleep on the gurney, only waking to urinate or to allow the stomach pump its ingress. Happy days. What will tomorrow hold?

Cheers!

Drinking Tips

Make friends with hopeless alcoholics: that way your drinking won't look as bad.

Befriend the porcelain god.
Most nights he will be your
only true friend.

Before you go out drinking,
always first line your stomach.
Scotch or vodka should do it.

The shakes: a reminder
that you ought to start
drinking earlier.

Arriving drunk at your first AA
meeting will only impress if you
buy a round afterwards.

If you drink a pint of
water before bed . . . it will
come out *in* the bed.

Drinkers' Comebacks . . .

Drunk? No, I always like to
park my car around a tree.

Pissed? No –
I'm a liquid bulimic.

Hammered? Don't think so –
anyway all these houses/
women/pets look the same.

Rat-arsed? I'll take you on,
and your twin.

Off my face? No – I *live* on
top of this bus shelter.

Legless? I suppose you'll be telling me that's *my* puke next.

Smashed? No – they suspended the laws of gravity in this pub.

Mullered? I'll have you know *everyone* is wearing traffic cones this season.

Shit-faced? I'm only letting you say that cos you're my best mate. No, wait, I hate you.

You Know It's Time To Go To Rehab When . . .

You've been declared legally dead at some point in the last twenty-four hours.

Someone said 'I do' and you did and you can't remember why or who or why we're in Vegas anyway.

You start to see why Anne Widdecombe might be considered attractive.

You have resident's parking
at the local A&E.

Mosquitoes die after biting you.

You wear an eyepatch because
it's easier to focus that way.

You forget your name at
the AA meeting – again.

You tip the ambulance driver.

Michael Barrymore calls
you up and tells you to
get some self-respect.

You tell so many people
'I'm not pissed' you actually
start to believe it.

The wine warehouse offers
you a loyalty card and
bulk discount.

You get done for driving under
the influence – in a dodgem car.

The weeks have got shorter
and you can't remember
the weekends.

A Short But Poignant History of Booze

Alcoholic beverages were discovered by accident. Primitive man tasted alcohol in fermented fruit and decided to improve on this strange new taste, except for farmers, who stuck with the rough cider. Booze can be produced from fruits, berries, flowers, honey, tree-sap, cactus, corn, barley, wheat, potatoes, grain and milk. Not your own milk.

Alcohol was a soothing substance to enable primitive man to escape the constant threat of a cold, hungry hostile world: that and nagging. The first hypocrisy was that severe intoxication was important to religious festivals and tribal ceremonies, but personal drunkenness is frowned upon. Therefore lots of other celebratory days were created. Like weekends.

Ancient civilizations used alcohol to welcome friends and take leave, to honour new leaders, New Year, marriages, births and deaths. They drank to launch ships, celebrate victory and to forget the misery and defeat of war. They drank in luxury and in poverty, to their gods and to earthly things. In short, same as today without the porky scratchings.

The ancient Egyptian priests
of 2300 BC price-fixed and
controlled the sale of
booze. Bastards.

Roman law was more
lenient about crimes committed
under the influence of alcohol –
for example, sleeping with
your mum and sister then
slaughtering the rest of
your family.

In the eighth century King Haakon the Good of Norway decreed that the midwinter celebration of yule was to be moved to December 25th. He said: 'Every man should have enough beer. And socks again.'

George Washington was a
devout beer-swiller. During the
American War of Independence
he proclaimed that the troops
would receive a daily quart of
beer. And if you've ever drunk
American beer you'll know that
you'll need at least a crate
to even get tipsy.

In eighteenth-century England, French wine was so heavily taxed that we learned to distil spirits. Soon the nation was permanently mullered on gin, which led to the government licensing drinking times and raising taxes. So you can blame the French for our licensing hours as well. Les Twats. Prohibition in America led to more drinking than ever before. Hey, let's ban sex!

NOSH

What to Eat With and After Your Beverage

FACT: 90% of all bar snacks have traces of urine on them ...

You have got to stop doing that.

Oh yes, drinking is enough, but there is often the need for sustenance too. Beer and wine may be your major food groups, but to co-exist happily with nature, you'll at some point crave the following more than life itself, you beered-up bloater.

FACT: Dinner is the best way
of making your incurable
alcoholism socially acceptable.

Porky Scratchings

You know you shouldn't.
You know they come from such
porcine cuts as cock, liver and
earwax, but you can't stop,
you weak fool . . .

Mini Cheds, Bacon Fries, Cheesy moments

So many E numbers they should make them illegal, or use them to spawn some new kind of rave culture.

Crisps

Instructions. Tear open packet. Spread astronaut-style reflective lining on table. Consume hungrily. Repeat until amalgam in teeth is replaced with imitation potato.

Bombay Mix

Direct from the floor
of local curry house.

Scampi Fries

Try these as an excuse for
why your fingers smell
of fish next morning.

Other dodgy pub snacks

Scotch eggs, pretzels,
urinal cakes.

Canapés

Posh pastry, sludge fillings
and tarted-up chipolatas so
middle-class people can
disguise their drink 'issues'.

Kebab

The original Greek tragedy.
You want salad? Yes – but only
so I can throw it across the
High Street. You want sauce?
No, I want to keep my tongue,
thanks. You like meat? I like the
crispy bits and not the grizzly
uncooked red stuff you get
when the spit isn't revolving
properly. You like pitta bread?
Isn't this some kind of
footwear? Am I eating
a sandal?!

Fish and Chips

Open or wrapped. With a
fishcake? (Hint. Fish and
cake are not two words that
happily sit in a sentence).

With saveloy. Ooh, it's all red
and long and fun to stick in
your zipper when the local tarts
walk in and say, 'Welcome to
the Saveloy Hotel – who
wants to book in?'

Vinegar? Yes, please – it's good on cuts and bruises.

Batter. God's way of covering up substandard fish product. Batter was originally broken away from the food and thrown away. Now it's the only part we really want to eat. Doesn't this tell you something?

Curry

After eight or more pints it's the law. If you're not sweating profusely and blasting what looks like Shredded Wheat out of your ringpiece for three days afterwards then you aren't really trying. Curry is now Britain's national dish – but only when it's dark.

And remember:

Poppadoms are not light frisbees.

All Indian waiters are not called
Sanjay, Garçon or Patel.

And they can piss in
your food as well.

Nan bread is not a flannel.

Takeaway containers
must apply to BS Standard
directive 637, which states they
are also capable of transporting
nuclear waste across the
country and whose contents
ought to be disposed of
in a lead-lined bunker.

The hotter the curry,
the harder the man.

Plan your runner effectively.
It's no good if you're so bloated
on pilau rice and chicken jalfrezi
that you only make the corner
before the waiter with the
machetes gets you.

Traditional English Breakfast

Guaranteed hangover cure.
Grease, dead animals and
fungus. That or the full
English. We repelled the
French, Huns, Danes and
Romans by going at it half-
arsed and tanked up. We were
fuelled by decent fry-ups.

Nowadays you have to pay upwards of six quid in the Granary for something that resembles the aftermath of nuclear war. And forget the 'Scottish restaurant' – breakfast was not meant to come on a muffin.

OTHER MEALS YOU MIGHT WANT TO HAVE WITH A BEVERAGE

Barbecue

In summer, we like to drag the food outside. You're safer necking the lighter fuel.

From 'barb' = bloke, and 'cue' = to ruin meat.

Instructions. Light fire. Drink. Watch meat burn. Drink. Throw away food. Drink. Set light to friends. Drink. Use remaining steak for eye injury.

Nuts

They make you drink more.
We like nuts.

Your last meal

OK, you were pissed, the
murder thing happened then
there was that stoopid trial and
now you're on death row. I
recommend the curry option,
along with ten pints and trying
to do a runner. Failing that –
you will leave behind a big
stink. Guaranteed.

Drinkers' Wisdom

Hangover: God's way of
reminding you how shit the
world is when you're sober.

Male friendship is
only beer deep.

You've had enough when
you realize you'd had
enough an hour ago.

Drinking alone is OK so long as
you can see imaginary people.

Who wants to live longer
than their liver?

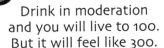

Drink in moderation
and you will live to 100.
But it will feel like 300.

You cannot be drunk in
charge of a lawnmower.

Enjoy the office party. It's
way of combining booze with
a kamikaze attitude to
employment.

If you can remember your
first drink you aren't
trying hard enough.

The hotel minibar.
Half the drink at
double the price.

The optimist sees the glass as half full, the pessimist as half-empty. I see it as your round.

All good drinking games should end up in casualty.

Memory loss. God's way of telling you . . . Something . . . I forget . . .

If God hadn't wanted us to drink, brawl, vomit copiously and soil ourselves he would never have invented minicabs.

The Lager Drinker's Prayer

'Alf a lager

Who art in Heineken

Hoegarden be thy name

Thy Kirin come, thy
Weatherspoon's be done

In Harp as it is in Amstel.

Forgive us this day
our Theakston's

As we forgive those
who tipple against us

Lead us not into temperance

But deliver us from Beamish

For thine is the Kronenburg

The Rolling Rock and
the Grolsch

For Stella and Stella

Bar man.

Low- and No-Alcohol Drink

There comes a time when you
realize that that crusty thing
left at the bottom of the glass is
you. And that for too long you
have been saying that water,
lemonade, tonic and soda are
poison. *Poison*, do you hear
me? So you tell people you're
going to cut down . . . order
twice as many halves, go to the
pub later . . . or even – not
drink. Then you will have to
come to terms with the
following . . .

FACT: Low-alcohol beer is about as much fun as *half* having sex.

FACT: When you are on the wagon you will realize that those leering, brawling, boring arseholes are actually your mates.

FACT: Detox is *not* about getting all that poisonous water out of your alcohol stream.

FACT: Tea is the most dangerous drink in the world. Look at the state of people who ask you for the price of a cup of it.

FACT: Low-alcohol drinks. So much time – so little fun.

Drunk Tests

Are you a bit of an alky?
A dipso? Try this simple test.
Any more than one correct
answer and you should
probably be leaving your
body to science right now.

❑ You have no qualms about
finishing the dregs because you
already have your eye on the
slops . . . and you're wondering
if it's OK to wring the beer
towel into your glass.

❑ Is the room moving up
and down? Are you
on a trawler?
If not . . .

☐ Your bottle-bank categories are clear, green and chaser.

☐ You believe everyone in the pub has an identical twin.

☐ You feel warm and wet between your legs and you're nowhere near a lady.

☐ You are the local drunk, but it's Scotland.

☐ How many fingers am I holding up? . . . Then fuck off, will you.

More Drinkers' Wisdom

Special Brew is God's way of reminding you that you're homeless and can't hold down a job.

Alcohol – so white people can believe they can dance.

Drinking buddies: people you rely on in a crisis, so long as the crisis occurs in a bar.

Beer makes you very sophis . . . sop . . . pisticated. Oh, sod it.

Ice: slows the pleasure –
diluates the pain.

Chasing the cigarette with your
wee should only be done when
the butt is *in* the urinal.

Break the ice at parties.
Start a fight in the coatroom.

Use alcohol like it uses you:
if you have the shakes –
become a cocktail barman.

There are two types of people. Those you drink with and those who you tell about it.

Blackouts – ideal excuse for missed birthdays, weddings, careers.

The magic words any drinker loves to hear: 'tickets', 'beer' and 'festival'.

There is nothing wrong with spending your holiday in a pub. It's why Torremolinos was invented.

Drink and Sex

Booze – it makes you want to slip into something hot, wet and meaty. Unfortunately, this will just be a kebab. Drink and desire have always gone together, and ended up locked out on the street at 3 a.m. Here are some tips about men, women and the magic liquid.

Men drink more than women because they lack the 'Y not' chromosome.

Women and beer: one has a good head, the other gives it.

The quickest way into a
woman's pants: charm,
money and good looks.
Failing that: vodka.

The perfect woman.
A mute with a 36-inch bust
who owns a bar.

Drink: so ugly people
can get laid as well.

Drink is like being in love.
Makes you deliriously happy,
leaves you nauseous.

What begins as wine, women and song ends up as beer, broads and brawling.

The difference between a pub and a clitoris? Any man can find a pub.

Try your luck. At a wine tasting, ask a woman if she spits or swallows.

Beer – dependant, down to earth, low maintenance – who needs women?

Of *course* beer bellies make us look pregnant. We're drinking for two.

Ladettes: Ladies who lose their lunch (or: ladies who lurch).

Your beer should be like your woman – deep, satisfying and containing 3 per cent yeast.

Never trust a beautiful woman in a sleazy bar. He's lying.

CELEBRATE – YOU'RE DRUNK!
Weddings, Parties, Funerals

Any excuse will do for swilling down gallons of the old amber liquid – but some are better than others. If you're lucky you can combine embarrassing friends and family simultaneously.

The Wedding

There is a far more communal
and meaningful event than the
joining together of two people
in holy matrimony, and this is
the joining together of several
men in the beered-up heaven
known as the stag night.
Or randy tarts and several
bottles of Archers and Malibu
on the hen night. Either way,
everyone will be showing up to
the do completely f**ked –
if they're lucky.

What You Need For A Good Stag Night

Passport.

Plastic – gold or platinum, preferably.

Handcuffs.

Stripper in improbable costume with unlikely story.

Shaving cream.

A tattooist.

Smart casual clothing.

Nappy for those little 'accidents'.

Map of whatever European destination you've ended up in.

Drink.

The Funeral

Showing up hammered at a funeral isn't strictly a mark of respect, though tippling from a flask is acceptable. A thermos flask is not.

If you fancy your chances with vulnerable women in black this might also be a good place to pull. Check if she's the widow first.

THE PARTY

We party for any
number of reasons.

Christmas is a wonderful
time for embarrassing
outbursts, naked photocopying
and proper hangovers.

New Year's is a time of wild
celebration, followed by an
avowed intent to better
yourself for the next day and
a half – or until the pubs open
– whichever is soonest.

Birthdays are always fun –
just remember the golden rule,
never ask how old the host is.
Even if she coquettishly
asks you to guess.

Gatecrashing – Three Simple Rules

1. Don't bring along four cans of Diamond White and claim to be a mate of Kevin's.

2. Don't push past the bouncer and point furiously at any name on the guest list. You are almost certainly not Elton John's boyfriend.

3. Don't drink anything out of an abandoned lager can that rattles.

Some More Tips
When Celebrating

The 'dodgy pint' is responsible
for more hangovers than
Christmas.

Surprise your friends and
relatives. Turn up sober to
your next wedding day.

Pass out on the dance floor.
Even party animals have
to hibernate.

Try Cinderella drinking.
Have a ball. At midnight
leave behind only empty glass.

There's always one who spoils
the party. If you've pissed your
kecks and punched the host
then chances are it's you again.

PUB TYPES

1. The pub kid. He's short, he's rude, and he's cadging money for fags or the fruitie. And he's the landlord's uncle's boy and you can't stop him.

2. The Antipodean barmaid. She looks like she'll put out. She's more likely to put your eye out. Australians may be the easiest lay in the world, but when you're the wrong side of the bar it ain't gonna happen.

3. The broken man. It's divorce or disease or something tragic. Either way he's not graced a Mr Byrite or hairdresser's since the Charlton combover was in style. He's got a story to mumble and if you stay his end of the bar long enough you're gonna hear it. Warning: it will turn your hair white.

4. The harpy. She's had her time and her memories and she's out for revenge. Don't worry – it's not you. Really. It's any man. Any *bastard man*!

5. Tramps. Why is it that women spend half their waking hours messing with their hair and it's us who loses it? Well – tramps don't. What their secret? Ask one. Go on. I double dare you.

Real Drinking Game no.1

Figuring out how a creaky weathered table with crisp packets stuffed in the slats surrounded by broken glass constitutes a 'beer garden'.

Real Drinking Game no.2

Putting the key in the lock. Shagging your wife before she wakes up. Finding your real home.

GREAT COUNTRIES IN WHICH TO DRINK

RUSSIA

If it makes you blind and you're not even touching yourself – it's Russian vodka! The average Russian downs forty-odd litres of vodka a year. And you wonder why Communism collapsed? They also drink perfume, disinfectant and brake fluid. Vodka costs next to nothing and Cossacks snort the stuff.
Well hard.

IRELAND

Drink Guinness. Why should the Irish have all the maudlin sentiment? The potato famine of 1845/46 may have given rise to the Troubles, but illicit booze was around long before that. The Irish mentality is so steeped in alcohol that they created the Celtic language and bog-thick accents solely with the idea of pissing off the English.

FRANCE

The French sip red wine and live to a ripe old age – and it looks it. Forget the Parisian honeys and look at those sun-beaten old prunes in Lyons. And if this is what they look like on the outside . . . Cirrhosis is a national disease and the national sport is boules – a game so blindingly stupid you could only play it when rammed. The French are permanently steaming – in pressed jeans and backpacks. They love a good riot, but lose wars. Not enough booze.
Try harder.

GERMANY

Colossus of lager production
and overconsumption. What
can't be said about the Germans
that isn't grossly insulting to a
nation with whom we waged
war over half a century ago?
Uhh, not a lot. Except they've
made up for it with great lager,
red-light districts and the
Oktoberfest beer festival.
Damn them.

UK

Warm beer and cricket?
That's for the Yanks. We all
know an Englishman's home is
his Castlemaine XXXX. OK, we
have still have useless licensing
hours and rip-off prices, but we
know how to drink. We know
what to drink and we know
that the fastest way to get
someone's leg's open is
to get 'em lashed.*

* *Especially northern bints
and posh totty.*

More Stuff About Drinking

Drinker's roulette.
When the room stops
spinning – bet on puke.

Drinkers' literature.
Tequila Mockingbird.
Oliver Twist (of lemon).
For Whom the Bells Toll.

Two words that will
tempt the most ardent of
abstainers: Free Bar.

Home brew. A drink for those too desperate to wait for fermentation.

Real ale. Brewed by fanatics, drunk by fakes.

Why we have licensing hours. Because twenty-four-hour drinking would kill us all in a month.

You are not a proper drinker unless you have had a fight in a pub, soiled a minicab and broken up at least one relationship – ideally in the same night.

The Welsh drink so much because of the mines. 'That one's mine ... this one's mine ...'

Things that sober you up fast. Blue light behind you. Purple lovebite seen by wife. Red piss.

Money – no, *beer* – makes the world go round (sometimes too fast).

Drinking buddies – because someone has to condone your sad, reprobate behaviour.

We all need a bar where everyone knows your name. 'Oy, *wanker*!!'

Caution: alcohol may cause street furniture to appear in your room.

How come happy hour is a magnet for miserable drunks?

Shaken, not stirred should describe your drink – not your state of consciousness.

Try and have the odd day off drinking. January 1st is popular.

Alcohol relieves stress.
More alcohol removes dress.

The drunkard's dream.
Owning a pub. Drunkard's
nightmare. The morning after
you bought the pub.

Why whisky is better than
vodka – you're too busy
fighting to be depressed.

Drinkers are like babies.
Bottle or breast – either is fine.

It took Jesus three days
to rise again. He had to sleep
off all that water.

Alcohol makes you depressed.
But then again – so does
the lack of it.

Look on the bright side of
your three-year ban. There's
more interesting stuff to
find/fall over/smash up
on your way home.

Sobering Up

Another quiz – because you like quizzes, don't you? That's one of your excuses for spending so long in the pub, isn't it? OK. Tick where applicable.

What type of drunk are you?
Happy [ ] Belligerent [ ]
Maudlin [ ] Vicious [ ]
If none of these apply,
try 'in denial'.

Are you the first in the pub
and the last to leave? [ ]
If you're not the landlord
or the pub dog then
you have a problem.

Have you ever known the
construction site in your head
to down tools and go quiet? [ ]
(NB: This is called being sober)

Did you know that sunlight is
warm – unlike neon and
fluorescent light? [ ]

Have you ever had a
conversation with a woman
that did not begin and end with
'Nice dress – what can I do to
talk you out of it?' [ ]

Did you know that there might be some women who are not bitches and some blokes who are not looking at you funny? [ ]

If so, you might want to think about laying off the sauce for a bit . . .

And finally . . .

The Drinker's Motto

I will never, ever,
ever do this again.

Ever.

And this time . . .

I mean it.

DR MARC BLAKE

Dr Blake is professor of Inebriate Studies at City University but may more commonly be found doing research in his local hostelry – the Cirrhosis and Firkin. A lifelong drinker, he was weaned on bottle and breast and refuses to leave them still.

As an undergraduate he was once arrested for being drunk in charge of a dodgem car – and for stealing the seventy-three miles of steel plating needed to get it home. He takes his work seriously, so much so that his laboratory contains a dartboard and snug bar.

Between blackouts he has managed to publish several papers, although some were used as hats. Something of a hellraiser, his ideal night out is with Richard Harris and Gazza, so long as they're paying. He was once married for a bet. He is at present working on an A–Z of vomiting. His ambition is to own a pub and to be called 'squire' for a bit. Until he pisses it all up the wall, anyway.